The Don't Laugh Challenge™

10 YEAR OLD EDITION

Don't Laugh Challenge
BONUS PLAY

Join our Joke Club and get the Bonus Play PDF!

★★★★★★★★★★★★★

Simply send us an email to:

bacchuspublish@gmail.com

and you will get the following:

- 10 BONUS hilarious jokes!
- An entry in our Monthly Giveaway of a $25 Amazon Gift card!

We draw a new winner each month and will contact you via email!

Good luck!

☺

★★★★★★★★★★★★★

Welcome to
The Don't Laugh Challenge ™

• How do you play?

The Don't Laugh Challenge is made up of 10 rounds with 2 games in each round. It is a 2-3 player game with the players being 'Jester #1','Jester #2', and a 'King' or 'Queen'. In each game you have an opportunity to score points by making the other players laugh.

After completing each round, tally up the points to determine the Round Champion! Add all 10 rounds together to see who is the Ultimate Don't Laugh Challenge Master! If you end up in a tie, use our final Tie Breaker Round for a Winner Takes All!

• Who can play the game?

Get the whole family involved! Grab a family member or a friend and take turns going back and forth. We've also added Bonus Points in game 2, so grab a 3rd person, a.k.a 'King' or 'Queen', and earn an extra point by making them guess your scene!

BILLY BOY

The Don't Laugh Challenge™ Activity Rules

- ## Game 1 - Jokes (1 point each)

  Jester #1 will hold the book and read each joke to
  Jester #2. If the joke makes Jester #2 laugh, Jester #1
  can record a point for the joke. Each joke is worth 1
  point. At the end of the jokes, tally up your total Joke
  Points scored for Jester #1 and continue to Game 2!

- ## Game 2 - Silly Scenarios (2 points each + bonus point)

  Without telling the other Jester what the scenarios say,
  read each scenario to yourself and then get creative by
  acting it out! You can use sound effects, but be sure not
  to say any words! If you make the other Jester laugh,
  record your points and continue to the next scenario.

  BONUS POINT: Get your parents or a third player, a.k.a
  King or Queen, involved and have them guess what in the
  world you are doing! Get the King or Queen to guess
  the scene correctly and you score a BONUS POINT!

The Don't Laugh Challenge ™
Activity Rules

Once Jester #1 completes both games it is Jester #2's turn. The directions at the bottom of the book will tell you who goes next. Once you have both completed all the games in the round, add your total points from each game to the Round Score Page and record the Round winner!

- ## How do you get started?

Flip a coin. If guessed correctly, then that Jester begins!

Tip: Make any of the activities extra funny by using facial expressions, funny voices or silly movements!

Jokes

How do farmers always know where their equipment is?

They use a GPS tractor!

/1

What fish has the smelliest face?

The SOCK-eye!

/1

How do researchers write essays?

With a pair-of-graphs!

/1

What TV channel is booming with viewers?

TNT!

/1

JOKES TOTAL: _____ /4

Silly Scenarios

(Act it out!)

Oh no, you've lost your voice! But, boy are you thirsty! Jump up and while in the air try to kick your legs forward like a dolphin to let everyone know you need a drink of water... STAT!

/2

Pretend you are a giant, scary dragon with a terrible cold. While taking a nap, you hear something and see that a knight accidentally woke you up. Let him know how grumpy you are!

/2

SILLY SCENARIOS TOTAL: _____ /4

NOW, PASS THE BOOK TO JESTER 2 ➜

Jokes

What do you eat for breakfast at the airport?

A PLANE bagel!

/1

What should you wear to a fireman's wedding?

A Soot!

/1

How's the traffic on Pinball Street?

It's bumper to bumper!

/1

What city wears a lot of sandals?

TOE-kyo!

/1

JOKES TOTAL: _____ /4

JESTER 2 CONTINUE TO THE NEXT PAGE ➡

Silly Scenarios

(Act it out!)

You are sitting outside and enjoying some fresh air, but the bugs won't leave you alone! As they start flying at your head, show what you do to get them to go away!

/2

You think you're taking a sip of soda, but turns out it has magic powers and turns you into a big grizzly bear! Act like a bear by walking on all fours, growling loudly, and chasing your friend around the room!

/2

SILLY SCENARIOS TOTAL: _____ /4

TIME TO SCORE YOUR POINTS! ➜

JESTER 1

$\dfrac{}{\textbf{ROUND TOTAL}}$ **/8**

JESTER 2

$\dfrac{}{\textbf{ROUND TOTAL}}$ **/8**

$\dfrac{}{}$

ROUND CHAMPION

Jokes

How did the tasty fruit lose their presidency?
They got Im-PEACH-ed!

/1

I met a woman named Ida Boofame. If I were her... IDA preferred a different name!

/1

What kind of salads were served on the Titanic?
ICEBERG Lettuce.

/1

What type of deer can you see through?
A win-DOE!

/1

JOKES TOTAL: _____ /4

Silly Scenarios

(Act it out!)

You are a very sleepy bird who keeps falling asleep while flying! Fly around the room and try to stay awake!

/2

You're driving a car that is automated. It accelerates, swerves, turns, and breaks when it chooses. You must act out a terrifying and outrageous ride in this car, who has a mind of its own!

/2

SILLY SCENARIOS TOTAL: _____ /4

 NOW, PASS THE BOOK TO JESTER 2 ➜

19

Jokes

My friend, Ray, is usually happy, but when he's sad, he calls himself Blu-Ray.

/1

What did the surgeon say to the scalpel?

"Cut that out!"

/1

What dance are corn chips best at?

Salsa!

/1

Why did the candy store owner decide his haircut looked funny?

/1

He kept hearing the Snickers!

JOKES TOTAL: _____ /4

JESTER 2 CONTINUE TO THE NEXT PAGE ➡

Silly Scenarios

(Act it out!)

You're taking a walk and you see a snake. You back away slowly, but he bites you and you have to hurry and suck out the poison to save your life!

/2

Pretend you're outside and it's **REALLY** hot out. Fan yourself using your hands, then dramatically melt onto the floor!

/2

SILLY SCENARIOS TOTAL: _____ /4

TIME TO SCORE YOUR POINTS! ➜

JESTER 1

$\dfrac{}{\text{ROUND TOTAL}}$ **/8**

JESTER 2

$\dfrac{}{\text{ROUND TOTAL}}$ **/8**

ROUND CHAMPION

Jokes

Knock knock.
Who's there?
Yurt.
Yurt, who?
You're too suspicious. Open the _____ /1
door!

Why didn't the tree go home?
It didn't want to LEAF!   _____ /1

Why did Luke Skywalker turn off the lamp?
He was a light-SAVER!   _____ /1

What culture loves boats?
The ROW-mans!   _____ /1

JOKES TOTAL: _____ /4

Silly Scenarios

(Act it out!)

You are a clumsy, cowboy gunslinger. Enter a duel and drop your gun when you draw! Kick it around a few times for effect!

/2
_____

UH-OH! You accidentally swallowed your phone and now it's in your stomach! Pretend to play on it, make calls, and use the touchscreen on your belly. Don't forget to make the sounds you hear on a phone, too!

/2
_____

SILLY SCENARIOS TOTAL: _____ /4

NOW, PASS THE BOOK TO JESTER 2 ➝

Jokes

Why didn't the tree know what to do after it was cut down?

It was STUMPED!   /1

What kind of peas look like they've been in a fight?

Black Eyed Peas.   /1

What fast food order describes an earthquake?

An extra-large shake!   /1

What did the yeast say to the dough?

"I'm only here to get a rise out of you!"   /1

JOKES TOTAL: _____ /4

Silly Scenarios

(Act it out!)

While walking in the garden, you spot some grapes, and decide to eat a handful... Turns out they are the **SOUREST** grapes you have ever tasted! Make your best sour face, then pretend to spit them out!

_____ /2

Act like a blind shark swimming around and trying to find some food, but every time you bite, you miss!

_____ /2

SILLY SCENARIOS TOTAL: _____ /4

TIME TO SCORE YOUR POINTS! ➔

JESTER 1

/8

ROUND TOTAL

JESTER 2

/8

ROUND TOTAL

ROUND
CHAMPION

ROUND
4

Jokes

What vegetable helps direct Broadway plays?

A CUE-cumber!

/1

Why couldn't the hair get off the island?

It was STRAND-ed!

/1

Why was the moth so motivated?

He wanted to be in the spot-LIGHT!

/1

Why was the sailor suddenly scared?

He heard a loud whale! (Wail)

/1

JOKES TOTAL: _____ /4

Silly Scenarios

(Act it out!)

While flying your kite, a seagull tries to steal it right out of the sky. Don't let it get away - reel it in with all your might as if you've got a big fish on the line!

_____ /2

You're an elephant on a rampage. Use your tusks and strong trunk to cause mayhem!

_____ /2

SILLY SCENARIOS TOTAL: _____ /4

NOW, PASS THE BOOK TO JESTER 2 ➡

Jokes

Why was the Jack-in-the-box so stressed?

It was tightly wound! /1

Why did the t-shirt only text his girlfriend?

It didn't like to COLLAR! /1

Why did the pig run away at dinnertime?

It didn't like what the owner was BACON! /1

What did the angry cake say to the boxer?

"You want a piece of me?!" /1

JOKES TOTAL: /4

Silly Scenarios

(Act it out!)

You feel the biggest sneeze of your life coming, you need to find a tissue quickly before it is too late! ACHOOO!!!

___ /2

You're a palm tree that got caught in the middle of a hurricane! Use your arms as the leaves and sway back and forth, like the wind is tossing you around!

___ /2

SILLY SCENARIOS TOTAL: _____ /4

TIME TO SCORE YOUR POINTS! ➔

33

 **JESTER 1**

/8
_____
ROUND TOTAL

 **JESTER 2**

/8
_____
ROUND TOTAL

_____
ROUND
CHAMPION

Jokes

Why are there so many headaches after a metal concert?

/1

Because everyone was headbanging!

When you need a package delivered, you rely on the mailman. When you have a bat problem, I guess you need... Batman.

/1

Why are tennis players such bad neighbors?

/1

They're always making so much RACKET!

What did the banana peel say to the psychiatrist?

/1

"I just feel empty inside."

JOKES TOTAL: _____ /4

JESTER 1 CONTINUE TO THE NEXT PAGE ➜

Silly Scenarios

(Act it out!)

A black hole has materialized in your living room, sucking up everything in sight as you struggle to escape! Hold onto anything and everything not to get sucked in!

/2

You have a very angry look on your face, but can't stop dancing! Don't you dare crack a smile!!

/2

SILLY SCENARIOS TOTAL: _____ /4

 NOW, PASS THE BOOK TO JESTER 2 ➡

37

Jokes

Why did the orange stay home from work?

It wasn't peeling well! _____ /1

Why do seagulls fly over the sea?

If they flew over the bay, they'd be BAY-guls! _____ /1

Where do feet go to dance?

The Foot-BALL! _____ /1

What kind of music does lead listen to?

Heavy Metal! _____ /1

JOKES TOTAL: _____ /4

JESTER 2 CONTINUE TO THE NEXT PAGE ➡

Silly Scenarios

(Act it out!)

You are a pirate sailing the ocean, but you lost your peg-leg! Hop around looking for it!

_____ /2

Pretend you are juggling a bunch of balls. Toss them into the air and look confused when they never come back down!

_____ /2

SILLY SCENARIOS TOTAL: _____ /4

TIME TO SCORE YOUR POINTS! ➜

 JESTER 1   /8

ROUND TOTAL

 JESTER 2   /8

ROUND TOTAL

ROUND
CHAMPION

ROUND
6

Jokes

What do geometry teachers and actors have in common?

They have to know their lines!

/1

What did the cow think of soy milk?

It was UDDER nonsense!

/1

Why did the self-driving car get glasses?

It had too many blind spots!

/1

What did the King say to his guards, before bed?

"Good KNIGHT!"

/1

JOKES TOTAL: _____ /4

JESTER 1 CONTINUE TO THE NEXT PAGE ➡

Silly Scenarios

(Act it out!)

You're a zombie on a shopping trip and you find the perfect shirt, but you can't seem to get it on over your zombie arms!

/2

While cooking burgers on the grill, you accidentally burn your finger. Ouch! Pretend to put a band-aid on and continue cooking, but then you burn yourself again... and AGAIN! Throw your spatula on the floor out of frustration and walk out!

/2

SILLY SCENARIOS TOTAL: _____ /4

NOW, PASS THE BOOK TO JESTER 2 ➡

Jokes

Why didn't the corn want to grow up?

It was afraid of being stalked. ___ /1

What did the wind say to the kite at takeoff?

"Just relax, it's a breeze!" ___ /1

What state has no pale people?

Mon-TAN-a! ___ /1

What do cats love to snack on?

A handful of GOLDFISH! ___ /1

JOKES TOTAL: ___ /4

JESTER 2 CONTINUE TO THE NEXT PAGE ➝

Silly Scenarios

(Act it out!)

You've just finished eating some delicious chips, but you look down and there are crumbs all over you! Yikes! Shake like a dog, from head to toe, to clean yourself off!

/2

Pretend you're a rattlesnake, slithering across the floor to sip on a nice, cold Coca-Cola. Give your best hiss, then drink through the straw!

/2

SILLY SCENARIOS TOTAL: _____ /4

TIME TO SCORE YOUR POINTS! →

JESTER 1

$/8$

ROUND TOTAL

JESTER 2

$/8$

ROUND TOTAL

ROUND CHAMPION

ROUND

7

Jokes

Knock knock.
Who's there?
Dim Sum.
Dim Sum, who?   /1
Dim some lights. You're
wasting electricity!

What kind of fruit is also good
at sailing?   /1
Navel oranges!

What do you call two fights
happening at the same time?   /1
Dual duels.

What did the apple say to the
peach?   /1
"Do you think we'd make a good pear?"

JOKES TOTAL: _____ /4

JESTER 1 CONTINUE TO THE NEXT PAGE ➡

Silly Scenarios

(Act it out!)

You're in a true test of courage, walking across the slippery, frozen ice cubes. Suddenly, tiny crabs start pinching your feet! HURRY! Get across the ice!

_____ /2

Beatbox while you do ballet! Be a beatboxing ballerina!

_____ /2

SILLY SCENARIOS TOTAL: _____ /4

NOW, PASS THE BOOK TO JESTER 2 ➡

Jokes

What do you call the average bully?

Mean.

_____ /1

Where do painters get their food?

From a CAN-vas!

_____ /1

What's the farmer's favorite sports team?

Dallas COW-boys!

_____ /1

What is the best finger food?

SNAP peas!

_____ /1

JOKES TOTAL: _____ /4

JESTER 2 CONTINUE TO THE NEXT PAGE ➡

Silly Scenarios

(Act it out!)

You are at the gym straining to lift a ridiculously heavy weight. While squatting, lift from the ground with all your might trying to pick it up, making your best under-pressure face! Then drop the weight and let out a sigh of relief!

/2

You're a superhero brushing your teeth, as you fly through the sky at the same time. Make sure to keep one hand out in front of you, so you can keep flying!

/2

SILLY SCENARIOS TOTAL: _____ /4

TIME TO SCORE YOUR POINTS! ➡

JESTER 1

/8

ROUND TOTAL

JESTER 2

/8

ROUND TOTAL

ROUND CHAMPION

ROUND
8

Jokes

Why was the elevator angry with its passengers?

They kept pushing his buttons!

/1

What is the initials of the baby's favorite state?

GA!

/1

Why did the pigeon get in the club?

Every-BIRDY is welcome!

/1

What is a lion's favorite condiment?

/1

Vine-GRRR! (Vinegar)

JOKES TOTAL: _____ /4

Silly Scenarios

You're in a rowboat, just rowing along. Suddenly, you see something scary and you *silently* scream! Start rowing as fast as you can by making circles with your arms to get away!!

_____ /2

You want to practice your first kiss, so you put some lip balm on and pretend to make out with your crush on your hand!

_____ /2

SILLY SCENARIOS TOTAL: _____ /4

NOW, PASS THE BOOK TO JESTER 2 ➡

Jokes

My mom used to hide the dictionary on top of our big screen TV. Now that's some **HIGH DEFINITION!**

_____ /1

Why was Coca-Cola a strict teacher?

It was SODA-manding!

_____ /1

Why did the cat stay home from school?

It wasn't feline well!

_____ /1

Which bird has the most extreme hair style?

The Mo-HAWK!

_____ /1

JOKES TOTAL: _____ /4

Silly Scenarios

(Act it out!)

You are a wolf howling at the moon, but you have a nasty cold. Try and howl, even though you keep coughing.

/2

Pretend you just twisted your ankle. So what! Dance on one leg!

/2

SILLY SCENARIOS TOTAL: _____ /4

TIME TO SCORE YOUR POINTS! ➡

JESTER 1

/8

ROUND TOTAL

JESTER 2

/8

ROUND TOTAL

ROUND
CHAMPION

Jokes

What two states work for the CIA?

North and South Decode-a!

/1

What was the foot's favorite nut?

The ca-SHOE!

/1

What did the construction worker eat with his fish?

TAR-tar sauce!

/1

Where does a fish choir perform?

At the choral reef!

/1

JOKES TOTAL: _____ /4

Silly Scenarios

(Act it out!)

You're a meditating monk that has a case of Spontaneous Disco Fever! They only last a few seconds, so try your best to keep meditating between dancing!

/2

Do your very best reenactment of a dog sledding leader, competing in a race. Don't forget to do your victory dance when you cross the finish line!

/2

SILLY SCENARIOS TOTAL: _____ /4

 NOW, PASS THE BOOK TO JESTER 2 ➜

Jokes

JESTER 2

Why couldn't the air conditioner go to the ball?

It wasn't FAN-cy enough!

/1

Why was the banana in 2 Fast 2 Furious?

They knew how to PEEL-out!

/1

What was wrong with the 89 degree angle?

It just wasn't RIGHT!

/1

Why was the heavy shoe so mean?

It was SOLE crushing!

/1

JOKES TOTAL: _____ /4

Silly Scenarios

(Act it out!)

It's hot outside! All of your friends are sweating buckets. Spin around, turning your head and flail your arms, like a human fan to cool them all down. Don't forget to make fan noises!

/2

You are mopping the floor when you get the urge to pretend you're the best rock star on the planet! As you're singing into your mop and banging your head, someone walks in! Try to gain composure, but instead pretend to slip and fall!

/2

SILLY SCENARIOS TOTAL: _____ /4

TIME TO SCORE YOUR POINTS! ➡

JESTER 1

/8
ROUND TOTAL

JESTER 2

/8
ROUND TOTAL

ROUND
CHAMPION

Jokes

What is a tree's favorite food?

OAK-ra!

/1

What do you call a short, Irish cat?

A Leopard-kan!

/1

What is Beauty and the Beast's favorite fast food restaurant?

Taco Belle!

/1

How do athletes measure their clothes?

In exer-SIZES!

/1

JOKES TOTAL: _____ /4

JESTER 1 CONTINUE TO THE NEXT PAGE →

Silly Scenarios

(Act it out!)

Pretend you're a penguin giving your best tap dancing performance! Be careful, the ice is SO slippery that it's almost impossible not to fall over!

/2

Unfortunately, you're afraid of walking. Travel around the room in any creative way you can think of, but if you have to walk, then pretend to be terrified!

/2

SILLY SCENARIOS TOTAL: _____ /4

 NOW, PASS THE BOOK TO JESTER 2 ➝

Jokes

JESTER 2

Why were the deer at the ATM?

To get a few BUCKS! ___ /1

Why does Sonic have all the bushes in town?

He's a hedge-HOG! ___ /1

What is Starbuck's favorite musical artist?

Ariana GRANDE! ___ /1

Why didn't the archer enter into the contest?

His arrows were broken, so it was pointless! ___ /1

JOKES TOTAL: ___ /4

JESTER 2 CONTINUE TO THE NEXT PAGE →

Silly Scenarios

(Act it out!)

You're paddling a boat around a lake while looking for a specific bird. Do your best bird calls and flap your arms like wings to get its attention!

/2

Sheesh, what a day! You're so tired, you have to let out a giant yawn. While you yawn, wave your hands by the side of your face to push out excess air from your mouth. Get rid of all the sleepy air, so you won't be tired anymore!

/2

SILLY SCENARIOS TOTAL: _____ /4

TIME TO SCORE YOUR POINTS! ➡

JESTER 1

/8

ROUND TOTAL

JESTER 2

/8

ROUND TOTAL

ROUND CHAMPION

ADD UP ALL YOUR POINTS FROM EACH ROUND.
THE PLAYER WITH THE MOST POINTS IS CROWNED
THE ULTIMATE LAUGH MASTER!

IN THE EVENT OF A TIE, CONTINUE TO THE ROUND
11 FOR THE TIE-BREAKER ROUND!

JESTER 1 _____
GRAND TOTAL

JESTER 2 _____
GRAND TOTAL

_____
**THE ULTIMATE
DON'T LAUGH CHALLENGE MASTER**

ROUND
11
TIE-BREAKER
(WINNER TAKES ALL!)

Jokes

What does a vegetable plumber do?
Fixes LEEKS!   /1

What did the woodworker like to eat?
Polish SAW-sage!   /1

What food always voted no?
Mayo-NAYS!   /1

What is a fish's favorite hot sauce?
Ta-BASS-co!   /1

JOKES TOTAL: _____ /4

Silly Scenarios

(Act it out!)

You're a brave and noble Knight, and you are in the middle of the hardest sword fight of your life! Around your back, under your leg, all around the room! Demonstrate the battle and victory!

_____ /2

Waddle like a duck across the room being careful to say "ribbit" with each step. Then turn around and hop like a frog across the room saying "quack" with each leap!

_____ /2

SILLY SCENARIOS TOTAL: _____ /4

 NOW, PASS THE BOOK TO JESTER 2 ➡

Jokes

Why did the furniture never fall down the stairs?

It was very CHAIR-ful!

/1

Why weren't the computers compatible?

They were wired differently!

/1

What kind of bird makes fun of people?

A MOCKING-bird!

/1

Which great lake do ghosts like?

Lake Erie!

/1

JOKES TOTAL: _____ /4

Silly Scenarios

(Act it out!)

Pretend you're a real-life Transformer. Zoom around the room with your arms stretched out like an airplane, then stop and move your arms and body to look like a robot, and start marching around the room!

/2

You're wandering in the desert and are SO thirsty! Crawl around and pant, while looking for some water!

/2

SILLY SCENARIOS TOTAL: _____ /4

TIME TO SCORE YOUR POINTS! ➔

ADD UP ALL YOUR POINTS FROM THE PREVIOUS ROUND. THE JESTER WITH THE MOST POINTS IS CROWNED THE ULTIMATE DON'T LAUGH CHALLENGE MASTER!

JESTER 1 /8
GRAND TOTAL

JESTER 2 /8
GRAND TOTAL

THE ULTIMATE
DON'T LAUGH CHALLENGE MASTER

Check out our

Visit us at
www.DontLaughChallenge.com
to check out our newest books!

other joke books!

If you have enjoyed our book, we would love for you to review us on Amazon!